D0041273

Books in Print by Marie Chapian

Teens:

>*Am I the Only One Here With Faded Genes?*
>*Feeling Small/Walking Tall*

Biography:

>*Back on Course* (Gavin McLeod Story)
>*Forgive Me* (Cathy Crowell Webb story)
>*Help Me Remember, Help Me Forget*
>*Of Whom the World Was Not Worthy*

Christian Living:

>*Close Friendships: Making Them, Keeping Them*
>*Free To Be Thin*
>*Love and Be Loved*
>*Mothers and Daughters*
>*Slimming Down and Growing Up*
>*Staying Happy in an Unhappy World*
>*Telling Yourself the Truth*
>*There's More to Being Thin Than Being Thin*
>*Why Do I Do What I Don't Want to Do?*

Devotional:

>*Discovering Joy*
>*His Gifts to Me*
>*His Thoughts Toward Me*
>*Making His Heart Glad*

Video:

>*Fun to Be Fit*

Discovering
Joy

Discovering Joy

Marie Chapian

BETHANY HOUSE PUBLISHERS

MINNEAPOLIS, MINNESOTA 55438

Scripture quotations are from the New American Standard Bible, © The Lockman Foundation 1960, 1962, 1963, 1968, 1971, 1972, 1973, 1975, 1977.

Published by Bethany House Publishers
A Division of Bethany Fellowship, Inc.
6820 Auto Club Road, Minneapolis, Minnesota 55438

Printed in the United States of America

Library of Congress Cataloging-in-Publication Data

Chapian, Marie.
    Discovering joy / by Marie Chapian.
        p. cm.
    "101 daily meditations for friends of God."
    1. Devotional calendars.   2. Joy—Religious aspects—Christianity—Meditations. I. Title.
BV4811.C4595   1990
242'.2—dc20   90-42101
ISBN 1-55661-122-6   CIP

To my new son
Eric Smith
who made my little girl,
Liza, his wife.

MARIE CHAPIAN, Ph.D. , is known around the world as an author and speaker. She also is a Christian counselor and a familiar personality to radio and TV audiences. She has written more than 25 books with translations in over two dozen languages.

Introduction

If you're like me, you need the Lord's wonderful Word every day; you need His voice, His presence, His loving guidance and blessing.

I am so honored to share with you the words of God in the simple way I've always heard from Him. With this fourth book in the A HEART FOR GOD devotional series, I am again thrilled and amazed at the depth of the love of God for His children. Through paraphrasing His Word in these 101 daily devotions, I have found a daily experience of *Discovering Joy* and breathing in His life. He is involved in every breath we take, every action, every thought. I marvel at the riches of His word, the beauty of His love, the sublime privilege of His discipline.

For years I have thought of the Bible as a personal love letter. In preparing these devotionals, my intention has been to allow His words to speak in such a way that we are drawn nearer to Him, closer to His heart of hearts. Even those times when His voice is stern, it is the tender voice of love. I believe there is no greater joy than knowing Him, loving Him and utterly bathing in His Word.

I pray with all my heart that these 101 devotionals will cause your heart to be filled with new understanding of yourself and your life, and that you will be refreshed with the everlasting and tender love the Father has for you.

I pray that He will speak directly to your heart through this book and that He will sweetly, personally, and unforgettably flood your heart with the desire to be *Discovering Joy* forever.

Day 1

These things I have spoken to you, that My joy may be in you, and that your joy may be full.

(John 15:11)

A moment's turning away from Me
   can be as a journey of a hundred years.
When you look longingly in another direction,
   mouth watering for forbidden fruit—
when you savor a sweet-soup temptation
   oblivious that the pot is scalding—
   you burn yourself.
Then you ask Me, "Why?"

I tell you, dear one,
   you are Mine, and you will always be
   Mine: I will never discard you.
Never will I turn My face from you,
   or leave you utterly alone.
You cannot shock Me.
   I never wring My hands,

or give you up.
Beloved, there is a longing,
a hunger in the Soul of souls
to see your heart released
from the allures
that will burn and scar you.
To see you set free
in the protective circle of heaven's Light,
illuminated by My endless love.
You were born,
not for the filth of life
but its beauty;
you were
born to love and live—
to discover joy.

John 16:1, 33

Day 2

*Cease striving and know that I am God
. . . Repent therefore and return, that your
sins may be wiped away, in order that times
of refreshing may come from the presence of
the Lord.*

(Psalm 46:10; Acts 3:19)

Why do you run from Me?
    You flee into the dismal
night of fear,
    you tremble at shadows,
imagine enemies.

I do not send you
    fire-tongued horrors;
I do not prepare steamy, dark paths
    on which you trip in murky potholes,
swallowed up
    by those around you, by your work.
It is not I who leads you in the way of
    emotional chaos.

Love does not misguide,
    or devour, make impossible demands.
Love does not burn
    the soul
    with unbearable trials.
Love liberates,
    renews,
        invigorates,
            enlivens.
And I am your love.
    Come back.

Psalm 46:1–2; Psalm 40:2; Psalm 17:7; Acts 3:19

Day 3

"Lift up your eyes to the sky,
Then look to the earth beneath;
For the sky will vanish like smoke,
And the earth will wear out like a garment,
And its inhabitants will die in like manner,
But My salvation shall be forever,
And My righteousness shall not wane."

(Isaiah 51:6)

It is not good
    to be cast down:
    That is not of Me.
Every injustice
    you suffer
shall be made sweet by Me,
    shall be transformed
    because you are
    precious to me
    and I love you.

If others do not live

as you want them to,
   it is My concern,
and I will bring to pass
   that which concerns Me.
Do not consider yourself
   higher than you ought:
   Pride will profit you nothing.
You are but a human being;
   I am God.
   I cannot fail.
I will never fail you.
   You will walk through all
   that I have purposed for you:
   Your experiences are important to Me.
Your heart is pure and holy and right
   when you are one with me.
My Spirit is able
   to accomplish every detail
   of every promise I have made.
Discover the joy
   of trusting Me.
Take joy,
   My beloved one,
   I love you.

Psalm 43:5; Jeremiah 31:3; Romans 15:15–16

Day 4

And He said to me,
"It is done.
I am the Alpha and the Omega,
the beginning and the end.
I will give to the one who thirsts
from the spring of the water of life
without cost."

(Revelation 21:6)

I am the beginning;
   I am the end.
You are very concerned with beginnings.
   You hesitate to reach
   the end.
The Alpha/beginning,
   the Omega/end,
   means that I am your all-in-all.
Do you want to stay
   an Alpha person—
   always at the starting line of faith?
That is a safe place—

where you *say* you believe Me,
where you champion truth,
but you don't move.

Move, I say!
Feel the wind of trials and
victories in Me.
I am the Finisher, the Omega.
Lift your eyes from the starting line
and focus on all that lies before you—
on the intelligent golden faith
awaiting you at the finish.

Learn of me; digest My Word,
always in communion with Me.
I am your health, your energy:
I bring you to a "finish"
that is not the end of all things;
not a place where you collapse,
emptied out, done.
It is the place where you
allow Me freely
to live through you.

My finish means new development,
new discoveries,
new victories,
new holy charges.

My dearest and most effective servants
    are those who move
    in "finished" faith.

Hebrews 12:2; Ecclesiastes 7:8; Acts 20:24; Isaiah 42:9

Day 5

But I do not consider my life of any account
as dear to myself, in order that I may finish
my course, and the ministry which I
received from the Lord Jesus, to testify
solemnly of the gospel of the grace of God.
(Acts 20:24)

"Finished" faith is Omega faith;
    it is living in the might I give you.
If you
    whine
    mope
    cry
    about things over which
    I have given you power,
    what use is that power?
Of what effect is your gift of faith?
You hide your power and do not use it.

I am telling you today,
Use the power I have given you!

Let your faith be the power
    that brings you to completion in Me:
Be whole in the name of My Son, Jesus.
Live in the Omega of your faith
    where there is no more groaning in defeat,
    only the triumphant practice
    of overcoming.
Discover joy
    in *all* things!

Dear one, keep your trust in Me
    and tell of all My works:
This is what gives Me joy.
For there is never cause
    for My little ones to despair,
    to fret,
    to give in to fearful imaginings.
Move on from your Alpha faith,
    and meet your peace,
your truest self
    in Me
    at the finish
    at the Omega of your faith.

*Revelation 1:6–7; Colossians 1:11–12; 2:10; Psalm 73:28;
2 Timothy 4:7–8*

Day 6

And without faith it is impossible to please
Him, for he who comes to God must believe
that He is, and that He is a rewarder of
those who seek Him.

(Hebrews 11:6)

Stand up,
    and take your place.
    Do the work I have called you to.
Pull down the strongholds—
    be brave, be strong!
Let Me teach you
    how to do My will;
Let Me be the love
    and the joy
that empowers you to act.
        Beauty is yours;
        power is yours;
        and peace that passes
        understanding.

Rise up; seek Me in faith.
   The time is now.

Psalm 143:10; Philippians 4:7; Matthew 7:8

Day 7

I will cry to God Most High,
To God who accomplishes all things for me.
He will send from heaven and save me.
(Psalm 57:2–3a)

I am with you.
I have never left you:
    we are one.

But you seek fulfillment in people.
    I want you to find
    fulfillment in Me:
Then I can bless
    your relationships with people.
And those amusements which tempt you—
    that seem so high and lifted up—
    they are only low places.
When you climb such "heights"
    you only scrape your nose
    on the bottoms of empty things.

My child, live where I live,
 hear My voice,
 know Me, enjoy Me.
Think *My* thoughts—
 bask in *My* attitudes.
I do nothing that is *un*-love;
 I do not withhold love.
Live with Me, above the emptiness;
 reach up and beyond the
 stunted, measured human heights.
If you want to fly,
 come soar the heights with Me.

Psalm 57:2–3; Hebrews 11:24–25; John 15:4; John 10:3

Day 8

The Spirit of the Lord God is upon me,
*Because the L*ORD *has anointed me*
To bring good news to the afflicted;
He has sent me to bind up the
brokenhearted,
To proclaim liberty to captives,
And freedom to prisoners.

(Isaiah 61:1)

I have chosen you
    to know My love in Christ
and to tell others of My love.
    You have much to learn.
But I make no mistakes:
    Your life is My message.
The longing world
    seeks love in stony, dark
    and loveless places.
People dying, alone,
    crying out to ears
    which cannot hear.

They grasp at
    arms which cannot comfort.
They remain unseen,
    unheard,
    unknown,
unloved.

I am more than a rescuer,
    I am life!
I am sure and true,
    forever loving.
And you, My chosen,
    shall know My heart,
    touch many lives.
Trust Me, trust Me.
    I live in you.

John 1:4; Isaiah 26:4

Day 9

For to me, to live is Christ,
and to die is gain.
(Philippians 1:21)

When you look
    only for blessings,
    only for answered prayers,
as the assurance of My love,
    you limit your experience
    of God.
My gift to you
    is the full vocabulary
    of life's poetry.
My gift is all the music,
    even the discordant phrases,
    and passages that are difficult
    and tragic.

When your prayers
    and service
are mere hopes of

worldly blessings
and rewards,
    discouragement becomes
your partner.

Can you be as thrilled with life
    and its stony paths
as you are with sunshine and flowers?
    My Spirit is bigger
than the world around you.

I want to give you the full measure
    of life's gifts,
    but you misunderstand:
        Trials are gifts from Me,
        changing you from glory to glory.
Never shrink from trials:
    I am your rock and refuge,
        a sheltering stronghold,
            a fortress.
Do not rely on the world
    for what you want.
    Oh, My dear one!—
I am what you want.

*Hosea 14:4; Psalm 91:9–11; 1 John 4:4; James 1:2–3;
2 Samuel 22:2; Psalm 71:1*

Day 10

I make you strong and healthy.
    Health is a gift from the Lord.
It is My desire
    that you bless your body.
Some of My children fight daily
    for their strength.
They struggle with disease
    and physical impairments.
My hurting ones
    are the apple of My eye,
    and My Spirit is in the midst
        of their pain.

Nourish your body:
    cherish your body
        for I cherish
    all of you.

There are those who receive
    only a swallow of food a day,
they do not have the luxury
    of choice.
You can choose to be a wise
    steward of your body:
Eat wisely,
    exercise wisely,
    sleep wisely.
Let your judgment
    be sound.

Exodus 15:26; Proverbs 4:20–22; 1 Corinthians 10:31;
James 1:5

Day 11

Or do you not know that your body is a
temple of the Holy Spirit who is in you,
whom you have from God, and that you are
not your own?

(1 Corinthians 6:19)

Keep the temple in which I dwell
    undefiled,
      by loving, thoughtful care.
I have many tasks for you
    and many roads for you to travel;
      never underestimate your calling.
Even in sickness
    I reign holy and supreme;
even in your weakness
    I am strong.
I am with you in every state
    of your physical being:
      when you are weary or full of vigor;
      when you are hungry or content with food;
      when you feel pain or pleasure.

Bless your body.
　　Do not despise it.
Do not insult it.
　　Respect it.
Learn what it needs,
　　how it functions best.
　　Your body is not your enemy.
I will show you
　　how to overcome bodily trials
　　and to make peace with the temple
　　I have given you.
Keep your heart young,
　　and full of hope;
　　your mind alert,
　　your senses alive.
Bless your body
　　and it will bless you
　　in return.

1 John 4:4; Psalm 103:1

Day 12

Keep a good conscience so that in the thing
in which you are slandered, those who
revile your good behavior in Christ may be
put to shame. For it is better, if God should
will it so, that you suffer for doing what is
right rather than for doing what is wrong.
(1 Peter 3:16–17)

If others come against you
    don't allow yourself to be tormented:
    Don't open yourself to inner agony.
You will never please all people,
    dear one.
You will make mistakes;
    at times
    you will offend others.
Misunderstandings abound:
    even good and right actions
    are sometimes misconstrued,
        goodness eyed suspiciously,
        righteousness repudiated.

Even My Spirit can go unrecognized.

Do not be shaken.
    Stand firm.
    Hold fast.
Allow yourself to be humbled before others.
    No evil spoken against you
    reaches My ears.

Galatians 1:10; 2 Thessalonians 2:15; 1 Peter 5:6

Day 13

Love covers a multitude of sins.

(1 Peter 4:8b)

I know your heart.
Yes! I know your heart.
  Do not be afraid of Me
  and My thoughts toward you.
My judgments are by My standards:
  I am love; I am mercy.
When you sense disapproval
  it is sometimes painful,
but I want to develop your character
  so that you are able
to withstand the fiery darts
  of the devil.

Your pride and anxiety of spirit
  are far more harmful
than rejection or gossip against you.
  Remember, My Son was the most
  hated of all men;

accused, despised, friendless.
Do not waste your emotions
    striving to defend yourself;
do not waste yourself
    on selfish fretting.
You crave recognition and approval
    from the wrong sources.

Center your thoughts,
    your emotions,
    on Me.
I make the sun to rise and set;
I can lift a soul
    from every pit of darkness;
    surely I will lift you up.
I am God, and there is no other.

Ephesians 6:16; 6:10; James 4:10

Day 14

And who is there to harm you if you prove
zealous for what is good?

(1 Peter 3:13)

I am the Beloved of all creation:
　　Lord of love,
　　Author of all things,
　　Giver of life.
If you would be held in high regard
　　in heavenly matters,
carry the banner of love:
　　wear an attitude of mercy,
　　let your hands extend forgiveness.
Honor and esteem
　　are among the affairs of heaven.
Your Lord and Savior never gossips,
　　never lies,
　　never points a finger
　　　　in harsh judgement
　　　　against His own.

The voice you must listen to is Mine.

    Do I condemn?

    Do I deride?

    Never!

I love with an everlasting love;

    I draw you to myself continually

    in lovingkindness.

When you abide in Me,

    evil words cannot destroy;

    rejection cannot tear down.

If you want approval,

    come to Me.

Psalm 12:6; 1 Peter 3:8–12; Psalm 95:6–9; Jeremiah 31:3

Day 15

I will sing to the LORD as long as I live;
I will sing praise to my God while I have
my being.

(Psalm 104:33)

I love your singing!
   Sing—it pleases Me.
Give to Me
   the song I give you.
All heaven dances and sings
   when you lift your voice
   and your instruments are sounded
      to bring Me praise and glory.
The angels sing and rejoice
   with you.
If you seek the admiration
   of others
   you will wear out
   with strife
      and frustration.
   If you live in the worldly shrine

of your talent you will strain and fret.
Flee from the youthful lust
   of hunger for recognition.
I do not require
   majestic voices;
I love
   the music of the heart.

Ephesians 5:19–20; Colossians 3:16

Day 16

It will no longer be said to you,
"Forsaken,"
Nor to your land will it any longer be said,
"Desolate";
But you will be called,
"My delight is in her,"
And your land, "Married";
For the LORD delights in you,
And to Him your land will be married.

(Isaiah 62:4)

I am with the fallen sparrow.
   I am with the lost, the lonely,
   the fearful, the weak.
      I am with you.
I am near to the humbled,
   the trembling, the sorrowful.
      I am near you.
I am in the saddened, wounded, forsaken.
      I am in you.

If you are without a cup for water,
or a friend,
if pain is your only companion,
if your heart is weary
and your mind dulled
by the battering storms of life,
I am your friend.

Your home in My heart
is warm and welcoming.
I caress you,
love you,
lift you up.
And when you gaze back at Me
in faith,
accepting My love,
I transform you:
All things become new.
I do this for you—
because you are
Mine.

Matthew 10:31; Psalm 34:10; John 15:15; 2 Corinthians 5:17; Revelation 21:5a

Day 17

*"But seek for His kingdom, and these
things shall be added to you."*
(Luke 12:31)

You may own the world,
   but you own nothing.
Those who lose all
   are those with the clearest eyes to see.
They are the ones who say,
   "Naked I came, and naked will I leave."
How little is yours
   without Me,
but how abundant your riches
   in Me.

My riches never pass away,
   never fade,
   never fail.

Where your heart is,
   there

is your treasure.

Philippians 3:8; Colossians 3:2; Luke 9:25; Job 1:21;
Luke 12:34

Day 18

*So also the tongue is a small part of the
body, and yet it boasts of great things.
Behold, how great a forest is set aflame by
such a small fire!*

(James 3:5)

Do not allow the words of your mouth
   to ensnare you.
Your words have power
   to hurt, destroy, kill.
They have the power
   to soothe, build,
     and to give life.
Do not allow foul or polluting language
   to come from your mouth;
     do not allow evil words.
Speak only what is good
   and helpful,
     kind,
     wise.
   Give grace,

love,
    beauty,
to all who hear your voice.
    Be a blessing.

Ephesians 4:29

Day 19

And my God shall supply all your needs
according to His riches in glory
in Christ Jesus.

(Philippians 4:19)

You complain of lack
    and needs unmet:
        I promise to supply
        all your needs
        according to My riches in glory.
You cringe in fear and weakness
    at the feet of a threatening world:
        I have not given you a spirit of fear
        but of power, and of love
        and of a sound mind.
You cast your eyes downward,
    telling others you are weak and poor:
        I am the Lord,
        the strength of your life.
Discover My joy.
    I renew your strength,

revitalize your life.
You will always triumph
in Christ Jesus.
You were born to be
victorious.

Philippians 4:19; 2 Timothy 1:7; Psalm 27:1;
2 Corinthians 2:14

Day 20

For you have not received a spirit of slavery
leading to fear again, but you have received
a spirit of adoption as sons by which we cry
out, "Abba! Father!"

(Romans 8:15)

Is there a prison strong enough
   to hold your spirit?
Is there a lie cunning enough
   to deceive your heart?
Where the Spirit of the Lord is,
   there is liberty,
      exultation,
         creative power.
You can do all things
   through Christ
      who strengthens you.
There are no walls
   high enough to imprison your faith,
no raging wolves powerful enough
   to tear apart your joy,

no thieves clever enough
　　to steal My gifts to you.
　　Walk in My Spirit.

Greater is the Spirit of God within you
　　than any evil in the world.
You have the power
　　to continually
live in freedom and in joy
　　as I continually
　　strengthen you.

2 Corinthians 3:17; Philippians 4:13; 1 John 4:4

Day 21

"Is this not the fast which I choose,
To loosen the bonds of wickedness,
To undo the bands of the yoke,
And to let the oppressed go free,
And break every yoke?"

(Isaiah 58:6)

Beloved,
    be gentle to those who are unkind,
    be loving to the unloving.
Touch and bless the world with hands
    which have been kissed
    by My love.
Embrace the ugly and the beautiful,
    presenting all to Me
    as a bouquet.
Lift up the heads which hang
    in despair;
open the gloomy gates,
    that the King of Glory
    may come into courts

where there has been only darkness.
Present Me. Sound the call.
Caress the downtrodden,
the homeless, the diseased,
the proud and the terrible.
Let the arms I love hold them.
Bring them
to My great heart
where they may find at last
a home.

1 Thessalonians 3:12; Galatians 5:13; Matthew 5:43–46;
Isaiah 12:4; Romans 15:1; Isaiah 58:6–8, 10

Day 22

Love is patient, love is kind,
and is not jealous;
love does not brag and is not arrogant,
does not act unbecomingly;
it does not seek its own, is not provoked,
does not take into account a wrong suffered,
does not rejoice in unrighteousness,
but rejoices with the truth;
bears all things, believes all things,
hopes all things, endures all things.
(1 Corinthians 13:4–7)

The servant of the Lord
    must not strive.

The servant of the Lord
    must not be jealous.

The servant of the Lord
    must war against these things,
    and be a strong warrior

ready to battle at all times
against contention, dissension,
disunion, schisms, rivalry,
belligerence and pride.

The servant of the Lord
must be meek, unselfish,
gentle, longsuffering
and mild,
bearing patiently with others
and making allowances in love.

The servant of the Lord
must be eager
to earnestly guard
and keep the harmony
and oneness
in the Spirit of God,
in the binding power of peace.

I never told you it would be easy,
but it is My will.

For I am the Father of all,
Sovereign over all,
pervading all,
and living in all.

I give My grace,

My unmerited favor to everyone
individually,
not indiscriminately,
but perfectly.
Will you be My servant?

1 Peter 3:15–16; James 4:6; 1 Peter 4:8b; Romans 4:16;
Ephesians 4:2–7

Day 23

. . . instructing us to deny ungodliness and
worldly desires and to live sensibly,
righteously and godly in the present age.
(Titus 2:12)

Turn away from youthful, foolish lusts—
   run from them.
Pursue righteousness—
all that is virtuous and good.
   I want you to think and act
   like Me
   in the sweet intelligence of My Spirit.
Never be quarrelsome:
Be kind to everyone
   and mild-tempered.
I can change the hardest of hearts,
   soften the cruelest nature.
Say goodbye to your old, self-defensive,
   angry disposition.
Put an end to it now—
   come alive in Me!

You can be confident in this:
   If you die with Me
      you shall live in Me.

As you become
   patient and forbearing,
   willing to suffer wrong,
   you will find great reward.
When you hear and obey My Word,
   you will see great miracles
   in the lives of those you touch.
My little one, come to your joy.
   Escape the jaws of the devil
and relax in My loving heart.

2 Timothy 2:22–24, 11, 26

Day 24

Cast your burden upon the LORD, and He
will sustain you; He will never allow the
righteous to be shaken.

(Psalm 55:22)

You labor hard and long
    and you bring forth good fruit—
    but your rewards seem few.
My heart's desire for you
    is hindered
    by such cares and worries.
Calm your anxieties and fears
    and enjoy My presence.
In quietness, seek My face;
    allow the light of My love
    to engulf you,
    warm you.
I will make a secret place,
    close to My heart
    where you will find me every day.
Then all you do

will reflect Me,
the One you serve,
and your troublesome burdens
will be no more.
Adore Me: I am your glory!
I am your breath and your being.
Lose yourself in Me:
I am the Lover of Souls!
Goodness and mercy follow you,
you are the light
of the world.
Shine.

Psalm 16:11; Psalm 23:6; Matthew 5:14

Day 25

*The earth is full of the
lovingkindness of the LORD.*
(Psalm 33:5b)

I have created a universe
    for you to enjoy;
I am the Source of its beauty.
    Relish the wonder of the earth
    as but a sigh of My glory,
    and be blessed.
New worlds of joy are yours
    in the discovery
    of My created things:
    See and learn.
You shall behold
    My love,
    deep, and deeper,
    at the heart of all.

1 Corinthians 10:26; Colossians 3:11

Day 26

Though I walk in the midst of trouble,
Thou wilt revive me;
Thou wilt stretch forth Thy hand against
the wrath of my enemies,
And Thy right hand will save me.
(Psalm 138:7)

Is there a heart so sad
    that I cannot make it rejoice again?
Is there a wound too sore
    for Me to heal?
Is there a soul so lost
    I cannot save?
All that is created,
    all that moves, crawls,
    thinks, dreams, soars,
    all that I have formed—
I watch over.
My love embraces
    the whole universe of created things;
    shepherding the hurting and misguided ones

into truth.
Never be shaken
    by the world around you:
Infinite love never fails.

Philippians 2:18; Psalm 68:19; 138:8; 57:3a; 17:6

Day 27

My soul takes refuge in Thee; and in the
shadow of Thy wings I will take refuge.
(Psalm 57:1)

Have I forsaken you?
  Never!
Pause for a moment,
  and open the eyes of your spirit.
What is the source of warmth and safety
  encircling you,
  caressing you, holding you?
What is this rich, resplendent protection
  that embraces you,
  its heavy, gold-threaded majesty
  too dazzling for the human eye to bear?
Dear one,
  you are wrapped in the robes of God.

Psalm 9:10; Psalm 121

Day 28

"When you pass through the waters,
I will be with you;
And through the rivers,
they will not overflow you.
When you walk through the fire,
you will not be scorched,
Nor will the flame burn you.
For I am the LORD your God,
The Holy One of Israel, your Savior."
(Isaiah 43:2–3a)

Do not be afraid of suffering.
You are born and nurtured by My Spirit,
    equipped for every situation:
Do not accept suffering
    as your lot in life.
You were born to overcome.
Understand this, in wisdom:
    You are in a transient world
        where evil abounds.
    You will never eliminate pain,

but it cannot defeat you.
No suffering goes unseen
by My omnipotent eye of mercy.
Suffering that is born with Me
must in time bring joy,
and deeper communion with Me.
Joy will not always reward
your activity in My service,
but it will come
when your suffering
is patiently and
bravely borne.

1 Peter 4:12–13; 2 Corinthians 12:9; John 16:33; Isaiah 61:7; Hebrews 2:10

Day 29

"And you shall love the LORD your God
with all your heart and with all your soul
and with all your might."
(Deuternomy 6:5)

Give to Me
    all that I deserve as God—
    all.
Your dreams,
    appetites,
        your thoughts,
        desires, and hopes.
Give all to Me;
    trust in Me
    perfectly.
Then you will know
    that I have come
    to love you,
    protect you,
    crown you with mercy
    and loveliness.

Give to Me your best
  and your worst.
  I, alone, turn mourning
  to dancing,
  ashes to gold.
I, alone,
  know your deepest heart.

Psalm 44:21; Psalm 139:23; Proverbs 3:5

Day 30

"Do not fear,
for I am with you;
Do not anxiously look about you,
for I am your God.
I will strengthen you,
surely I will help you,
Surely I will uphold you with My righteous
right hand."

(Isaiah 41:10)

I want you to be called
   strong.
Be ready to handle
   snags and hindrances.
Prepare yourself to be
   full of My grace.
Understand what patience means.

I want you
   to inspire and emenate goodness;
      to live in honesty,

67

to handle the unmanageable,
    solve the unsolvable,
    calm the unruly,
    love the unlovable.
No one can accomplish these
    by human strength.
But you are able
    because you and I are *one.*
Do not miss the joy
    of discovering My abilities in you.
        Live your life as a miracle,
        even in imperfection and chaos
live each moment
        as a unique event.
    There is life and purpose.
Live in Me,
    and you live the miracle.

Zechariah 4:6; Philippians 4:13; Colossians 3:12;
Romans 10:12–13

Day 31

The wise in heart will be called discerning,
And sweetness of speech increases
persuasiveness.

(Proverbs 16:21)

Nothing is too small
    for Me.
I am in the big events,
    and in the very small.
    There is not a sigh too soft
        that I cannot feel it;
        not a cell or microbe too small
        for My presence to give life.
    Do not overlook the tiny things.
Listen for My still small voice,
    the voice no crashing storm can cover.
Hear Me in the stillness of the night,
    in the voice of a cricket,
    in the quiet sigh
        of a newborn child.
Hear Me. See Me.

I am in all things.
It is the eye brightened
    by My Spirit
    which finds Me
in the very, very
small.

Psalm 131:1; Isaiah 30:21; 1 Kings 19:13b

Day 32

We shall know by this that we are of the truth, and shall assure our heart before Him, in whatever our heart condemns us; for God is greater than our heart, and knows all things.

(1 John 3:19–20)

You are so hard on yourself.
You are surprised
   at your own imperfections;
you agonize
   when you discover flaws and blemishes
   in your character:
Listen, for I have something to tell you.
You are Mine, and you are
   growing,
   learning,
   changing,
   developing
into an ambassador for Christ.
You do not win more of My heart

by beating your breast,
by insisting how "terrible" you are.
Repentance is what I desire;
not self-loathing.
Do not be deceived
by foolish religious rituals
meant to impress man,
not God.
I know the human frame,
I formed you perfectly,
so that you would perfectly fit
into Me.
You make My heart glad
when you quietly take My hand
and together
we handle your humanity.

With My hand in yours,
overcome
and respect yourself.

2 Corinthians 5:20; 1 John 2:12; John 15:5; Romans 8:37

Day 33

*"For the mountains may be removed and
the hills may shake,
But My lovingkindness will not be removed
from you,
And My covenant of peace will not be
shaken," says
the LORD who has compassion on you.*
(Isaiah 54:10)

Do not impose limitations on Me.
   Do not lock Me away
   inside the gates
   of your fears and habits.
Secretly, you believe
   that you will always live a life of lack;
this is like binding yourself
   to a burning post.
You are called to *live*—
   to live *abundantly*!
You have *all* things in Me;
   you can do *all* things through Christ:

Multiply your talents,
improve your life.
You are not defeated.
I paid for your well-being
by the sacrifice of My Son, Jesus.
It is time to discard
old ways of thinking.
I, your Father in heaven,
know all your needs before you do.
I have provided much for you.

Today be lifted up
above the sorrows of yesterday.
Today, receive new vision,
new hope, and new strength.
Limit me no longer:
Never put a limit on the blessings
I have for you.
It takes courage
to take more of God,
more of the blessings of God.

Romans 5:10; Matthew 6:8, 32; Isaiah 54:17

Day 34

"Now therefore, O sons, listen to me,
For blessed are they who keep my ways.
Heed instruction and be wise,
And do not neglect it.
Blessed is the man who listens to me,
Watching daily at my gates,
Waiting at my doorposts.
For he who finds me finds life,
And obtains favor from the LORD."
(Proverbs 8:32–35)

Your gifts to Me
  are lovely.
Never imagine that someone "better,"
  more prominent,
might render your gifts
  less significant to Me.
    I love the cup of cool water,
    as I love the faith in a lion's den.
    I love the woman judge, leading Israel to
      victory;

and I love the humble ones,
    weeping at the foot of the cross.
Your gifts to me are as fragrances
    in My garden of joy.
To look upon your face
    and love you,
knowing you are Mine
    and knowing your adoring heart
is more precious
    than a thousand festivals in My honor,
is My delight.

Love Me in simplicity.
    Give all that you do to Me.
    Talk to me,
    listen to Me,
    worship Me.
And find your life
    exciting.

*Luke 21:1–3; Matthew 10:42; Daniel 6:16–22; Judges 4:21;
4:9; Luke 23:27; Colossians 3:17*

Day 35

*Stand still and consider the wondrous
works of God.*

(Job 37:14)

Take My hand,
   let Me hold yours tenderly.
Let Me sit with you
   in the silence.
      Alone, you and I,
      let us remain perfectly still.
With your heart locked in Mine,
   let us enjoy
   one another.

Isaiah 32:17; Psalm 23:1–3; Hebrews 3:14

Day 36

But as for me,
the nearness of God is my good;
I have made the Lord God my refuge,
That I may tell of all Thy works.

(Psalm 73:28)

Do you know how precious
    these quiet moments are
    to Me?
Do you know how beautiful
    you are to Me,
    and how I long to speak to you?
Do not deny yourself the luxury
    of these silent moments
    with your God.
In just one moment with Me,
    you bring more contentment
    to your soul
than all the good works
    your skills can accomplish.
One moment alone with Me;

one moment out of a busy day;
one moment to enter into the presence
    of complete perfection—
    sitting at the center
of the sheltered peace of God—
    this is the best thing moment
of all.

Psalm 32:7; Philippians 4:7; Ecclesiastes 9:17; Psalm 4:4

Day 37

How beautiful you are,
my darling,
How beautiful you are!
(Song of Songs 4:1)

Inner beauty can be counterfeited
    for a time
But then the temper flares up
    and you snap at life
        as one without hope.
You make an excuse:
    "I'm just tired today."

My beauty can become in you
    an eternal quality,
    glorious and indestructible.
    Nothing can mar it.
        No moment's agitation
        can spoil its sweetness;
        no irritation
        can pollute its quiet composure.

Beauty is the reflection
of the moments and hours
you spend with Me.
You are beautiful to Me.

Proverbs 31:30; Song of Songs 4:7; 1 Corinthians 13:12

Day 38

Therefore if any person is in Christ, he is a
new creature; the old things passed away;
behold, new things have come.

(1 Corinthians 5:17)

And as I forgive you,
  dear one,
  so you ought also
  to forgive yourself.
It is good to deny yourself
  the folly of a self-centered life.
It is good to recognize
  your self-centered thoughts and actions,
  and to repent of them.
To be dead to sin and selfishness
  means to live at last—
  to *live*, clean and beautiful,
  in Me.
Only then can you be satisfied
  in your inner being.
Only then can you walk in forgiveness,

freely pardoning all
who sin against you.

I forgive,
    I restore,
        I make new.
And in Me, dear one,
    all is well.

Hebrews 10:22; Philippians 4:7; Micah 7:18

Day 39

For you will go out with joy,
And be led forth with peace.
(Isaiah 55:12)

Joy and peace are in Me:
    There is little satisfaction
    in attainments apart from Me.

Do not let *doing* take first place
    over *being*.

Attainments, accolades, awards and prizes
    pass away and are forgotten—
    but our relationship remains.

Your reward lies far beyond
    temporary flattery,
    and human gratitude.
When you are one with Me
    our achievements dance around us

like jewelled children.

2 Corinthians 4:18; Ephesians 6:7–8; Daniel 12:3;
Isaiah 51:11

Day 40

How much more will the blood of Christ,
who through the
eternal Spirit offered Himself without
blemish to God, cleanse
your conscience from dead works to serve
the living God?

(Hebrews 9:14)

What is a good conscience?
   One that has been armed
   with joy and truth.
      Why would a person
      settle for less;
      remaining spiritually lacking,
      and emotionally impoverished?
Put on the full armor of God
   so that you may be equipped
to fight off the enemies
   that would rob you of
   the good life.
A good conscience reminds you

when you need Me.
A good conscience tells you
　　to take more of the Holy Spirit,
to let the Word of God empower you
　　to be live bravely.

Dare to be a happy person!
　　Dare to be strong.
　　Dare to overcome!
A good conscience—
　　one that rejoices in truth—
　　is ever confident,
　　is at peace in adversities.
A good conscience
　　is like gold.

*2 Corinthians 1:12; 1 Thessalonians 5:8; Ephesians 6:11;
6:10; Revelation 3:21; Hebrews 10:22*

Day 41

Count yourselves dead to sin,
but alive to God
in Christ Jesus.

(Romans 6:11)

The glory of a godly person is a good conscience.
   It brings deep and lasting gladness.

An evil conscience
   is always fearful and upset:
   Wicked people have no peace.
      Evil people will never
      experience true joy.

But you, dear one,
   considering yourself
dead to all that is not of Me,
   are alive and at rest.
Your happy heart will laugh
   and you will discover your world
   to be filled with delightful

surprises.

To the pure all things are pure.

Isaiah 57:20–21; Titus 1:15; Proverbs 22:1; Isaiah 13:12

Day 42

But whoever wishes to become great among
you shall be your servant.

(Mark 10:43)

Take me with you today
    wherever you go.
I will calm your unsteady nerves;
    I will remind you
    when you are self-righteous.
I will gently nudge you when you boast,
    when you become self-important.
I will set your feet
    upon the path of true fulfillment—
        which means to intelligently
        lose all things
        so that you may gain
    much more in Me.

Philippians 3:8–9; Luke 12:2; James 1:5; Job 8:20; Mark 8:35

Day 43

Those who trust in the LORD
Are as Mount Zion,
which cannot be moved,
but abides forever.

(Psalm 125:1)

If you do not trust another,
   why should one trust you?
Secretly, you do not trust Me.

You continually look for signs—
   for acts of devotion,
   for words you hope are true.
What use is your quest?
   Many religious people
     play their pious roles
     like actors on a stage.
   Don't be tempted
     to join their show.
Stand upon My holy hill,
   with clean hands

and a pure heart that trusts.
You will never trust another,
    or yourself,
    until you learn this:
        Trust in Me.

Proverbs 3:5; Proverbs 29:25; Psalm 24:1–3

Day 44

Then our mouth was filled with laughter,
And our tongue with joyful shouting;
Then they said among the nations,
"The LORD has done great things for them."
The LORD has done great things for us;
We are glad.

(Psalm 126:2–3)

Learn to laugh;
    learn to hear the glory of God's laughter!
The Lord does not wince with worry.
I am God!
    I am wisdom and knowledge.
    You can trust Me.
Do you think you can light a fire of worry
    in your heart
    and not be burned?
Do you think you can linger
    on the hot coals of anxiety
    and not be blistered?
Put an end to your troubles, I say,

and take My words into your heart.
In them you will find
   peace for your troubled heart.
      Enter, by My words,
         into My loving heart
         and remain there.

Psalm 126:5–6; Revelation 1:8; Psalm 33:21; Proverbs 6:27–28; Isaiah 26:3; Proverbs 7:1–2

Day 45

I will lift up my eyes to the mountains;
From whence shall my help come?
My help comes from the LORD,
Who made heaven and earth.
He will not allow your foot to slip;
He who keeps you will not slumber.
Behold, He who keeps Israel
Will neither slumber nor sleep.
(Psalm 121:1–4)

Who is your helper in time of need?
   Who lifts you up,
   who vindicates you,
   who hears your cries in the night?
Your employer?
   Your lover?
      Your friends?
Who is always there—
   covering you, protecting you,
   embracing you in perfect love?
Who calls you Beloved?

Your neighbors?
    Your parents?
        Sisters or brothers?

Is there a human being who can give you
    eternity?
Are you born-again through
    romantic pursuits?
        Marriage?
            Childbirth?
Is your soul washed white as snow
    because of educational accomplishments?
    because of social successes?
Whom do you worship, My dearest one?
    to whom do you credit
    your blessings?
People come and go—
    success is temporary,
    riches are fleeting.
But God is from everlasting to everlasting.
    I do not change.
    I am yours forever.

Hebrews 13:6; 1 John 4:16; 1 Timothy 6:17;
Psalm 148:13–14

Day 46

If anyone fiercely assails you
it will not be from Me.
Whoever assails you
will fall because of you.
. . . No weapon that is formed against you
shall prosper;
And every tongue that
accuses you in judgment you will condemn.
(Isaiah 54:15, 17a)

Enemies?
   Who can raise a finger
   against God's elect?
   Who dares to rattle their tongue
   at My chosen ones?
When you put *Me* before *you*,
   you need not contend
   with troubling words.
People may belch out insults
   with their mouths,
slash at you with sarcasm and ridicule.

What is that to you?
I am strength, wisdom and power.
  I will cause you
    to look triumphantly upon derision,
    which is nothing more than weeds.

I alone am your defense;
  sing praises to Me.
You have My loving approval;
  you need nothing more.

Jeremiah 32:17, 27; Psalm 59:7, 9–10

Day 47

But as for me, I shall sing of Thy strength;
Yes, I shall joyfully sing of Thy
lovingkindness in the
morning,
For Thou hast been my stronghold,
And a refuge in the day of my distress.
O my strength, I will sing praises to Thee;
For God is my stronghold,
the God who shows me
lovingkindness.
(Psalm 59:16–17)

Where do you run for safety?
　　Under the table,
　　or to My heavenly high tower?
Where do you run for help?
　　To the pharmacy,
　　the supermarket,
　　or to My mercy which lasts forever?
In My holy refuge
　　there is peace

and steadfast love.
It is easy to forget the One
who protects you—
is it not?

Isaiah 53:6; Psalm 59:9, 16–17

Day 48

Do not be eager in your heart to be angry,
For anger resides in the bosom of fools.
(Ecclesiastes 7:9)

I rule the surging sea;
    When its waves mount up
    I still them.
I still the turmoil of nations;
    and I make the voice of the strong
    a mere whisper.
I rebuke the wind and the lightning;
    the hail, snow and clouds
    do My bidding.
Who has gone up to heaven
    and come down?
Who has gathered up the wind
    in the hollow of his hands?
Who has wrapped up the waters
    in his cloak?
Who has established
    all the ends of the earth?

What is His name?
  Tell me if you know.
I, the Lord of all,
    gave the sea its boundary,
    so the waters would not overstep
    My command.
I marked the foundations
    of the earth . . .

. . . and I can quiet your disturbed heart.

Allow Me rule your mind
    as I rule the seas,
    as I rule the wind,
    and the earth.
Give your tempestuous fears
    to Me,
    and like calm, glassy waters,
      so will I make
    your soul.

Psalm 65:5–7; 89:9; 107:29; Matthew 8:26; Proverbs 30:4

Day 49

But you shall receive power when the Holy
Spirit has come upon you; and you shall be
My witnesses both in Jerusalem, and in all
Judea and Samaria, and even to the
remotest part of the earth.

(Acts 1:8)

Stop saying you have no power.
Be as the prophet who said,
"—as for me,
    I am filled with power,
with the Spirit of the Lord,
    and with justice and might—"

I have armed you with strength,
    it never runs out.
You are one who can soar
    on wings like eagles,
you can run and not grow weary,
    you can walk and not be faint.
Do nothing out of fear.

Never be dismayed.
I am your God.
Fear is not your god.

Speak the truth to your heart:
I, out of My glorious riches,
will strengthen you with power
through My Spirit.
Never say you have no power.

Micah 3:8; Isaiah 40:31; 41:10; Ephesians 3:16–17a

Day 50

Pursue peace with all men, and the
sanctification without which no one will see
the Lord.

(Hebrews 12:14)

Do not accuse a person,
    when he has done you no harm.
It is a fool who is eager
    to quarrel.
Like one who seizes a dog
    by the ears
    is one who meddles in a quarrel not his own.
Concentrate on the task I give you;
    rule your own heart,
    and do nothing out of selfish ambition.
Consider even those who offend you
    as better than yourself.

Proverbs 3:30; 20:3; 26:17; Philippians 2:3

Day 51

Then you will call, and the LORD will answer;
You will cry, and He will say, "Here I am."

(Isaiah 58:9a)

Yes, it may seem that I am not answering
    soon enough.
        You find yourself in the valley
        of patient waiting
        (although you are not altogether
        patient there.)
    You feel as though you're trapped,
        with no way out.
Never forget My promises are sure.
I never go back on a promise,
    and I will surely
    answer you.
But dear one,
    I answer in My time,
    not yours.

Isaiah 25:9; Psalm 91:15; Isaiah 65:24

Day 52

Do not forsake your own friend or your
father's friend,
And do not go to your brother's house in
the day of your
calamity;
Better is a neighbor who is near than a
brother far away.

(Proverbs 27:10)

Moses grew weary—
    and who was it who lifted up his hands?
    Do not neglect your friends.
Aaron and Hur held up Moses' hands,
    one on one side,
    one on the other,
so that his arms remained steady
    till sunset.
Friends will do this for you.

You are well-loved,
    and the love you show to friends

will bear much fruit.
Live in harmony with your friends,
     be sympathetic,
     compassionate,
     humble.
Always remember:
     You were born to
     love and be loved.

Exodus 17:12; 1 Peter 3:8; 1 Samuel 18:1; Proverbs 17:17a

Day 53

But I say, walk by the Spirit, and you will
not carry out the desire of the flesh.
(Galatians 5:16)

I want you to be
   self-controlled.
Be alert!
   Do not slip into foolishness.
   Look down and see where you are standing.
Is your foundation sound?
Your enemy the devil
   is prowling around
   like a roaring lion
   looking for someone
   without self-control
Whom he may devour.
But you have a rock,
   Christ,
   on which to stand.

1 Corinthians 10:12; 1 Corinthians 16:13; 1 Peter 5:8

Day 54

For in hope we have been saved,
but hope that is seen is not hope;
for why does one also hope
for what he sees?

(Romans 8:24)

Be filled with hope!
Take hold of hope
    as never before,
    and know
        that the Maker of heaven and earth,
        the Maker of the seas,
        and everything in them
        is faithful to you forever.

Hopelessness is a lie,
    and lies last but a moment.

The truth lasts forever.
    I give you a new hope today,
a promise that I am in your prayers,

near you, hearing you,
answering.

Romans 3:4; Hebrews 6:18; Psalm 146:6

Day 55

Acquire wisdom; And with all your acquiring, get understanding.

(Proverbs 4:7)

If you are wise,
 wisdom will reward you.
Wisdom is My gift to you:
 Joy is impossible
 without it.
   When you wander about,
    looking for happiness
   in the toothsome grins
    of strangers,
   you are deceived.
Live unto Me;
 you belong to Me.
Look for Me first,
 and My kingdom.
   My kingdom is filled
   with delights for the soul.
   My righteousness is sweet

and fills your longing heart.
All things will be added to you
    when you seek wisdom.
This gift is yours.

Proverbs 9:12; Romans 14:8; Matthew 6:33

Day 56

Sow with a view to righteousness,
Reap in accordance with kindness;
Break up your fallow ground,
For it is time to seek the LORD
Until He comes to rain righteousness on
you.

(Hosea 10:12)

Think of yourself
   as a planter.
Think of yourself
   as one who plants righteousness—
      that is, uprightness
      and right standing with Me.
When you are firmly planted in Me,
   you reap in mercy
      and lovingkindness.
It is time to break up your uncultivated ground
   for now you must find Me,
   be one with Me;
   it is time to be My friend

114

and not an alien in your own land.
Think of all that you do as a field
    where you plant good seed.
Let Me rain good things upon you.

Hosea 10:12; Galatians 6:8; James 2:23; Ezekiel 36:27

Day 57

Arise, shine; for your light has come,
And the glory of the LORD has risen upon you.

(Isaiah 60:1)

Awake, dear one.
   Clothe yourself with strength.
Awake, and take the robes I give you.
Awake, and live this day in wisdom
   and integrity.
Don't hide the loveliness of My truth,
   but put it on like a garment.
My Spirit of truth in you
   makes you to shine.
I will give
   and give
      to you today:
   Your eyes will be opened,
   your body strengthened,
   your mind refreshed,
   and your heart cleansed.
Walk in the light;

I am the Light.

1 Thessalonians 5:8; Matthew 13:43; 1 John 1:7a

Day 58

But godliness actually is a means of great gain, when accompanied by contentment.
(1 Timothy 6:6)

Choose, today:
Decide to appreciate your life,
   as it is right now.
Stop hunting among shadowy substances
   from the past,
     to explain your troubles today.
When you do this,
   you give the past
   power to rule the present;
   you miss the majesty of *this* moment.
Introspection can be destructive,
   like a rushing river in a storm,
   flooding all in its way.
I want you
   to love your life,
   to put aside
     complaints and grievances

                    which are like annoying
                    pounding waters.
Your discontent
    bites like fleas
but the contentment
    I give is a warm
blanket of love.
    You are sweet
in My eyes.
    Be at peace.

Ephesians 5:8; Titus 3:3; Romans 14:11

Day 59

The beginning of strife is like
letting out water,
So abandon the quarrel before it breaks out.
(Proverbs 17:14)

Delight yourself in the spiritual victories of others:
　　Delight in all triumphs
　　in Christ Jesus.
Rejoice when another's success is greater than yours:
　　Be glad when another receives
　　what you need.
Remain at peace when another receives the attention
　　you think you deserve.
You must not strive:
You must war against
　　all jealousy and conention.

Say *today*:
　　I will not be jealous.
　　I will not contend.
　　I will not strive.

I will rejoice at another's victories.

I will delight in the success of others.

I will not think others less worthy
or less important than I.

I will not see my work as more important
than someone else's.

I will pray for those who are my competitors.

I will rejoice in my relationship with the Lord.

And so it will be.

2 Corinthians 12:20; Mark 10:43–44; Galatians 5:26;
2 Corinthians 2:14; John 13:34

Day 60

Then the glory of the LORD went up from
the cherub to the threshold of the temple,
and the temple was filled with the cloud,
and the court was filled with the brightness
of the glory of the LORD.

(Ezekiel 10:4)

You have been created by Me
 to go forth into life
with great openness of heart—
 to embrace life.
When you thank Me for the dark moments
 and for those events that crush—
 when the powers of evil seem nearly victorious—
you will breathe a prayerful thank you
as My Spirit whispers,
 "It is well."
When a dark hour descends
I will make you rise up, furious as a lion,
 and leap upon the enemy,
 in My name.

My Spirit will accomplish this.

The saint of God must know
    when to fight,
    and when to be still.
I speak to you of *discernment*—
    of unlocking your limited human vision.
Let your spirit live
    in a greater consciousness of My will.
Let My will cohabit your will,
    like a penetrating light,
    giving you clear vision on all sides.
When your will becomes one with Mine,
    I prepare your mind with truth
    concerning all events of life.
Daily training in My Spirit's vision
    will make you
    like a rock beside a storm-driven sea,
    unshakable.

Zechariah 10:5; Ecclesiastes 3:5; 1 Peter 1:3–8; Psalm 17:15;
Proverbs 4:13; Hebrews 6:1

Day 61

*He has made everything appropriate in its
time. He has also set eternity in their heart,
without which man will not find out the
work which God has done from the
beginning even to the end.*

(Ecclesiastes 3:11)

Be sensitive today
    to My presence
    in the world around you.
Let My Spirit awaken your senses
    to the sublime,
    to all natural beauty.
Smell the rose with deeper joy,
    watch the scurrying of a bug
    with greater amusement,
    feel the wind as a friend.
Put your hands on the earth; experience its pulse.
    Loving My world
    is a form of humility
    because you must put

124

your inner conflicts aside
to communicate with life outside yourself.
Can you appreciate the sunlight streaking
across a wall?
Can you see great art in rivers of rain
marking a dusty window?
If your heart is over-powered
with the drumbeat of worry,
you will miss the anthem of a sunset.

You'll miss My sigh of love.

Psalm 139:7–10; 16:11; 65:9–10; Luke 12:27–30

Day 62

Teach me to do thy will, For thou art my God; Let thy good Spirit lead me on level ground.

(Psalm 143:10)

The words I tell you
    are easy to understand,
    guiding your life in Me.
These "simple," daily words
    guide you into the profound mysteries
    of eternal life.
Grow strong in My words,
    and become an arrow of faith,
    flying from the heart of Glory.
        My Word is Spirit and Life,
        healing the sick,
        giving sight to blind eyes.

I am He who fashioned the heavens
    and stretched the waters into seas:
I will speak to you day and night,

if you have ears to hear.
I will show you great and wonderful things;
    I have created you
    for My purposes.
Do not lose your way, trying to make happen
    that which you are not called to do.
When your ways please Me,
    even your enemies
    will be at peace with you.
To do one thing without Me
    is unnatural and unbearably lonely.

Know My will.

Psalms 40:8; 2 Peter 1:4–11; 1 Corinthians 2:9; Isaiah 46:10;
Psalm 100:3; Proverbs 16:7

Day 63

> *But if any one does not provide for his own,*
> *and especially for those of his household, he*
> *has denied the faith, and is worse than an*
> *unbeliever.*
>
> *(1 Timothy 5:8)*

It is far easier to admire those
   who are far away from you,
   than those in your own midst.
It is far more convenient
   to be kind to a troubled stranger,
   than to an unruly soul
   of your own household.
I have created you to be
   as I am,
   living in the skill of love.

Love is at the root of all I am,
   and you must learn its language
   through My Spirit and My Word.
Spend much time meditating in love,

and practicing love.
Love is not an accident.
Love is kind first of all
    to your own family
    and those who are closest to you.
Love ignores no one,
    insults no one,
    takes no one for granted,
    refutes no one,
    crushes no one.

Today, love those nearest you—
    with patience, thoughtfulness,
    warmth and prayer.
I expect it of you.
    They need you.

Ephesians 4:32; Romans 12:10; 1 John 4:16; Psalm 127:3

Day 64

The steadfast of mind
Thou wilt keep in perfect peace,
Because he trusts in Thee
Trust in the LORD forever.
(Isaiah 26:3–4a)

It is a sure promise:
    I take care of the helpless and poor
    when they cry to Me;
I care for the weak and needy
    and I rescue them;
I save you from oppression
    and from violence.
Because your life is precious to Me
    I want you to live!
        I want you to prosper,
        to enjoy abundance.

Honor the name of My Son forever.
    His name will continue as the sun
    and all will be blessed in Him,

all nations will praise Him.
I am a good God
and I am good
to you.

Psalm 72:12–15; Psalm 73:1

Day 65

The LORD is in His holy temple; the
LORD's throne is in heaven; His eyes
behold, His eyelids test the sons of men.
(Psalm 11:4)

I see those arrogant ones—
   whose pride dangles at their necks,
   whose fine clothing is woven of cruelty and deceit.
They do not know the present life they live
   is but a dream.
They will awaken and find
   to their terror,
they have nothing.
   Sleek and fat,
these proud ones walk a soft road now,
   boasting in their riches
and their talents.

But you have been born again!
   No more is your present life a dream.
You have found the glorious truth.

Do not fret yourself
nor be dismayed and confused
     at the prosperity of evildoers.
My eye is ever watchful
     and nothing escapes My gaze.

I have rescued you
     and I will continue
     to rescue you.
Remember my gaze.

Proverbs 21:6, 17; 2 Thessalonians 2:10; 2 Corinthians 5:17;
Jeremiah 23:23–24

Day 66

But truly I am full of power by the Spirit of the Lord.

(Micah 3:8a)

You are beginning a new path today.
    Lavish yourself in My love.
    Clothe yourself in My love:
        Dwell in it,
        live by it,
        put on the love of God.
Love is the beginning of wisdom,
    and your path requires wisdom.
    Have compassion today;
    let mercy go before you.
In My love
    Know that I am God.
    I am the One who guides you;
    I am the One who has called you.
    You are not too old for the task ahead,
    not too inexperienced,
    not too weak.

You are *empowered*.
Listen to your heart.
Tell yourself,
until you truly understand:
"I can do *all* things through Christ
 who strengthens me."

Proverbs 4:18; Colossians 3:12; 1 Timothy 1:12;
Philippians 4:13

Day 67

For the word of the LORD is upright;
And all His work is done in faithfulness.
(Psalm 33:4)

My love is the energy
   keeping the world
and the glory of the universe.
   Love is at the core of all
that lives.
It is foolish
   to reject the love of God.
Take the excellence of My love
   and let Me be known in You.
My love is the path of life.

Move steadily forward—
   learning,
   ever learning
   of Me,
   ʼays in pursuit of the essential.

You, My beloved,
    are My showcase,
    the recipient of My love,
    the one to whom I reveal and give
    My true self.

1 John 4:16; Deuteronomy 10:12–13; Psalm 32:8; Matthew 6:33

Day 68

For you have been bought with a price:
therefore glorify God in your body.
(1 Corinthians 6:20)

What does your life mean
   to you?
Is it your heaven-on-earth,
   dedicated to pleasing Me?
Do you live to glorify Me,
   to give *all* to Me?
Are you wholly
   devoted to My glory?

What else in the world
   can yield the satisfaction
   you have in
   living unto Me,
     pleasing Me,
       doing My will?

The greatest truth of life

is this
and always will be:
I am your life.

1 Peter 4:11; Acts 17:24–25

Day 69

I delight to do thy will, O my God;
Thy Law is within my heart.
(Psalm 40:8)

Never judge your life by the limitations of time:
The Lord Jesus was thirty years old
    before entering His public ministry,
and He ministered but three short years.
    When He died on the cross
there were still millions of souls
    who remained unreached,
        untaught,
            unhealed.
But in His holy example
    of obedience and love,
    He glorified Me perfectly.
        Time does not limit Me:
        A moment is as a thousand years.
Your task is to discover and complete My will
    no matter how long
    or how short a time

it takes.

My Son completely fulfilled My will,
    unrestrained by the boundaries
        of time.

Fix your goals of excellence on Me,
    not on the work itself—
    and never on *time*.

Your life is to fulfill My will:
    This is the ecstasy we share.

Psalm 143:10; Philippians 2:8; Matthew 26:42;
Philippians 1:9–11

Day 70

Whether, then, you eat or drink or
whatever you do, do all to the glory of God.
(1 Corinthians 10:31)

If you sit down to eat
    at a sumptuous banquet,
    or if you nibble at tasteless crumbs—
when you eat, eat for Me.
If you drink of exotic elixirs
    from golden goblets reserved for kings,
    or if you lap water from your hands—
when you drink, drink for Me.

Whatever you do:
If you sleep till the noon sun
    bakes your bed,
    or if you rise up early
    before the dew;
if you work around the clock,
    earning little except
    the joy of your labor;

if you dance with the moon,
  sing with the stars,
if you bring soup to the sick,
  and grain to the poor,
    whatever you do, do for Me.

Work, play, laugh, cry—
  and love Me—
  first.

Romans 14:6–8

Day 71

You are the light of the world. A city set on a hill cannot be hidden. Nor do men light a lamp, and put it under the peck measure, but on the lampstand; and it gives light to all who are in the house. Let your light shine before men in such a way that they may see your good works, and glorify your Father who is in heaven.

(Matthew 5:14–16)

You are the light of the world.
  Imagine the great cities of the world
  in all their lighted splendor—
  suddenly gone black.

I am in you:
  My Holy Spirit fills you,
  ignites you,
  and is impossible to quench.
I *will* be known in you.
  Be glad your light shines

for all the world to see.
Take joy that your good works
    are seen
and that I, your Father,
    am glorified in you,
and I am proud of you.

Matthew 5:13–16; Psalm 43:3; Acts 13:47; Philippians 2:14–16

Day 72

And the Spirit and the bride say, "Come."
And let the one who hears say, "Come."
And let the one who is thirsty come; let the
one who wishes take the water of life
without cost.

(Revelation 22:17)

The word I speak to every living soul is
    "Come."
I want to carry the burdens that
    weigh so heavily on your shoulders.
I want to teach you the skills of
    rest,
which means to leap into My lovingkindness
    as you would plunge into cool waters
    on a hot day.

Those who refuse
    to give their burdens and cares to me
    find nothing but exhaustion.

If you will just come to Me with every burden,
    your life's circumstances will unfold
    like a flower,
and you will discover
    the joy of My purposes.
Come: Give Me your weariness.
Come: Give Me your sins.
Come: Give Me your labors.

I will give you rest as sweet as honey,
    its lovely taste refreshing,
    renewing your spirit
every moment.

Matthew 11:28; Isaiah 55:1; Psalm 26:3; Matthew 11:29–30

Day 73

For I am the LORD your God,
who upholds your right hand.
Who says to you,
"Do not fear, I will help you."
(Isaiah 41:13)

You can be happy—
not because you are without problems,
   but because you can be certain
      I meet you in the center
      of every problem.
Though there are troubles
   on every side,
      you will not be perplexed.
Though you find a "wolf"
   behind every tree,
   ready to attack your flock,
      you will not despair.
Defeat will never be
   the song you sing;
   worry will never be your companion.

You will not rise up in vengeance,
    and anger will remain
    far from you.
You will handle your life
and all its snares and troubles
    in the love and wisdom
    of the God you serve.
You will shine in darkness!
    Walk in truth!
        You will live to see
            My beautiful countenance
as your own.

2 Corinthians 4:8; Psalm 55:22; Proverbs 20:22

Day 74

Heaven and earth will pass away but My words will not pass away.

(Luke 21:33)

You are in need of the knowledge
   of My Word.

When the light of knowledge
   comes through My Word,
   faith is the result.

Pray for illumination,
   so that the Holy Scriptures
   will breathe life to you
   and infuse your entire being
   with My mind and will.

Your faith will multiply
   when ignited by My Word.

My Word is spirit and life.

Treasure My Word more
    than your daily bread;
    My Word will be
    your heart's delight.

John 6:63; Job 23:12; Jeremiah 15:16

Day 75

The grass withers, the flower fades,
But the word of our God stands forever.
                                    (Isaiah 40:8)

My Word is eternal
    and stands firm in the heavens.
Heaven and earth will pass away
    but not My Word.
My Word is a magnitude of light
    that waits to pass through
    your mind and soul and body.
It is the glory of God
    to feed your soul,
    precept upon precept,
perfect, whole, sound,
    until you are transformed
        into My image.

Come to me
    through My Word.
Read. Understand.

Dedicate yourself to daily study
of the Scriptures.
I will do more than guide you,
I will caress you with confidence
I will feed you with knowledge.
My Word is a lamp for your feet
and a light for your path
forever.

Psalm 119:89; Matthew 24:35; Isaiah 28:10, 13;
Psalm 119:105

Day 76

You shall therefore impress these words of
Mine on your heart
and on your soul; and you shall bind them
as a sign on your
hand, and they shall be as frontals on your
forehead.
(Deuteronomy 11:18)

How do you keep your way pure?
  By living according
  to My Word.

And how do you know My Word?
Only by the illumination of My Spirit
  will a person know
  the power and depth
  of My Word.

My Word, made alive by My Spirit,
  transforms the ignorant,
  and the proud;

creates wisdom,
where there was once
only dullness.

My Word makes you clean
and beautiful.

Come to My Word;
wash yourself
in love.

Romans 10:8; Psalm 119:9; 19:7; John 15:3

Day 77

But if any of you lacks wisdom, let him ask
of God, who gives
to all men generously and without
reproach, and it will be
given to Him.

(James 1:5)

A wise person is one who has
    understanding and mercy.
A wise person has compassion
    and endeavors
    to understand
    the ways of other people.
If you will be wise,
    give your energies
    for the benefit of others.

You long to know so many deep things
    of My Spirit.
And I hear you.
My words to you are many,

My thoughts toward you
   are as the sand of the sea.
I want to instruct you in the ways of wisdom.
I want to lead you tenderly
   with My perfect wisdom
   and My love.

Proverbs 4:5–10; Acts 20:35; 1 Peter 4:11; Jeremiah 29:11

Day 78

Who may ascend into the hill of the LORD?
And who may stand in His holy place?
He who has clean hands and a pure heart,
Who has not lifted up his soul to falsehood,
And has not sworn deceitfully.

(Psalm 24:3–4)

Keep yourself pure for Me.
   I see your goings and your comings.
I watch over you like a mother hen.
   You are engraved on the palms of My hands
   and everywhere you go
you take Me with you.
Let your soul delight in
   the ways of honesty and integrity.

My Spirit is a great consuming fire;
   He gently guides and nudges you
   to do the right thing.
There is nothing concealed
   that will not be disclosed;

there is nothing hidden
   that will not be made known.
Hidden faults are not to be
   swept beneath the bed;
they are to be confronted
   and given to Me,
   so I can wash you clean.
I will help you
   develop strong character.
Let My Spirit and My Word
   be your teacher
   and Physician.

Luke 12:2; Ephesians 5:11; Psalm 19:9–13

Day 79

And so, as those who have been chosen of
God, holy and beloved,
put on a heart of compassion, kindness,
humility, gentleness and patience;
bearing with one another,
and forgiving each other,
whoever has a complaint against any one;
just as the Lord forgave you,
so also should you.
(Colossians 3:12–13)

A person without compassion
   is like a well without water,
   like a bowl of dust,
   to one who is thirsty.
A person without compassion
   is a bag of nails
   scattered on a soft bed.

Weave compassion
   tightly into your heart.

Compassion does not repel or brush aside.
It does not grow hostile with rebuke;
it is never rude.
Compassion never judges harshly,
nor is it quick to condemn.
The grace of God is Christ.
The mercy of God is Christ.
The compassion of God is Christ.
And Christ came to give
all to you.

Matthew 25:35–40; Proverbs 19:17; Hebrews 2:16–17; Psalm 145:9

Day 80

Be it done to you according to your faith.
(Matthew 9:29b)

I want you to be aware
of the unlimited power you have
when you exercise your faith.
The faith you demonstrate
makes full proof of Christ's supremacy
over all.
Faith is
the proof of the resurrection of My Son
and the reality of the Gospel.
Faith grows,
expands with use;
it honors Me by believing
My precious promises.

You have the power within you
by the same Spirit that raised Christ
from the dead
to perform mighty acts of faith.

Do not deny yourself
the power of miracles in your life
    and in your world.
Never say you don't have enough faith—
    because faith the size of
    a grain of mustard seed
    is all you need.

Put your faith to use
    as never before.
I charge you to go into the world and:
    Pray for the impossible.
    Trust Me for answers.
    Believe.
    Move mountains.
    Bring Me pleasure.
    Be a success.

James 2:17; Matthew 25:14–29; Matthew 17:20;
2 Chronicles 20:20; Mark 11:22; John 6:28–29;
Hebrews 11:6

Day 81

The LORD is good,
a stronghold in the day of trouble,
And He knows those who take refuge in
Him.

(Nahum 1:7)

When the future seems dim
    and your mind can form no bright ideas
    of a better world,
concentrate on Me:
    I am your Father who loves you,
    and I am good to you.

Don't let a heavy heart shake your composure:
    I am your Father who loves you,
    and I am good to you.

You are surrounded by My goodness:
    goodness before you,
    goodness following you.
Look for My unfailing love

as it overruns the world
and spills into every corner.
Though your head may hang low,
and your hands flop sadly at your sides,
you are standing in the center of a
glowing sphere of heavenly goodness.
Lift your face!
Taste and see!

Your Father loves you,
and is good to you.
In joy and in suffering,
I am good to you.
In sweetness and in sorrow,
I am good to you.
In life and in death,
I am good to you.
Think about
My all-surrounding goodness.

Psalm 25:8; Psalm 33:5; Psalm 34:8

Day 82

Bear ye one another's burdens, and so fulfill the law of Christ.

(Galatians 6:2)

How heavy is your burden?
   Can you, beneath the weight
   of your own burden,
   lighten the burden of someone else?
When you complain that the veil of trouble
   is too thick around you,
   that you cannot feel My lovingkindness;
   when you bemoan
   that you cannot do anything right—
how can you help anyone else?
You are never so helpless that
   you cannot give help.
You are never too lame
   to lift up another,
never too blind
   to help another find the proper path,
never too groggy of mind

to tell another
of My amazing love.
In spite of your complaints
I am always blessing,
loving and protecting you.

Jude 1:22–23; Acts 20:35

Day 83

In quietness and trust is your strength.
(Isaiah 30:15b)

Quiet your heart.
　Listen for the small desires
　of your heart and Mine.
　　Listen for our thoughts
　　to melt together,
　　forming a perfect union.
With me, you will discover untold joy
　in the smallest sigh of life.
Nothing is insignificant to Me.
　Listen to the sweet urgings of
　My will for this new day.
It is the restless heart
　that demands grand and monumental events.
Listen for the silent things.
　Cherish the simple.
I work slowly and do a work perfectly in you.
　If you do not love the minute,
the almost imperceptible,

you find yourself fermenting
in impatience and frustration.
  It takes many years of discipline
to turn a mortal being
    into an immortal one.
Enjoy each moment
    as a gift.

*Psalm 4:4; John 15:11; Philippians 1:6; Numbers 9:8;
Romans 2:7*

Day 84

At the acceptable time I listened to you,
And on the day of salvation I helped you;
behold, now is the acceptable time,
behold, now is the day of salvation.

(2 Corinthians 6:2)

Your concern for the future
    beats at you like driving rain
    on a blossoming flower.
Soon the torrents
    will bow your head down,
    you'll lose your fragrance
    and you will be
    wilted,
    soggy,
    frayed.
It's a condition you created yourself.
Your storm of worry was not ordained by Me.
    Won't you end this tempest?
    Won't you live *today*?
You struggle to manipulate life's

eventualities
and all your efforts bring
frustration and despair
because you cannot control
the actions of God.
You *can* know the mind of Christ,
(though you cannot *control*
the mind of Christ).
Leave tomorrow to Me, dear one.
Live for today.

Matthew 6:27; James 4:4; 1 Corinthians 2:16

Day 85

*O Lord, open my lips, and my mouth will
declare your praise!*

(Psalm 51:15)

When you accept
   the goodness I give to you
   and you are at last satisfied—
   give Me praise.
Praise Me in silence
   and in awe.
Praise Me in thankful whispers;
   praise me in noise.
Praise Me with harp, lyre,
   dance and drum.
Praise the Lord
   using your creativity.
I have opened the gates for you.
   Enter as though you were leading
   a long procession
of jeweled and robed saints.
   Pass the tall carved pillars

along the golden promenade
   and enter My sacred courts
   with thanksgiving and praise.
Dancing, singing and gladness
   fill My house,
   as your praise fills My heart
and My joy fills
   all of heaven and earth.

Deuteronomy 8:10; Psalm 33:2; Psalm 100:4

Day 86

Yet Thou art He who didst bring me forth
from the womb;
Thou didst make me trust when upon my
mother's breasts.
Upon Thee I was cast from birth;
Thou hast been my God from my mother's
womb.

(Psalm 22:9–10)

Your birthday is a special day to Me.
　　When I considered your birth
　　I took many things into account:
the time, the climate, the events of the day,
　　the lives of those whose world you'd share.
I considered all these things,
　　and finally sent you to the world
　　　　to be:
　　to take your place among the living,
　　and to live your days for Me.
I purposefully gave you
　　the life you have,

in order to fulfill the plans
    I have for you.
You were not born too early; nor too late.
You were born perfectly on time.

I decreed the very day, hour, and moment
    when you would enter the world—
    tiny, blinking and wet.
Can you still hear the angels,
    and the welcome song they sang?
They sing over you today—
    and every day of the year.
Your heavenly Father
    Who gave you life
kisses you on the nose.
Happy Birthday!

Ecclesiastes 3:2; Isaiah 44:2; 43:7

Day 87

The Lord is not slow about His promise,
as some count slowness,
but is patient toward you,
not wishing for any to perish
but for all to come
to repentance.

(2 Peter 3:9)

How deep is your wound, dear one?
Anchor your spirit in Mine:
    I will rejuvenate;
I will pour out the warm oil
    of inner strength.

Live the winged life,
    above the cares
that rob your soul
    of flight.
Fly, soar to your waiting joys!

No longer count the scars,

but the prayers I've answered
all along the way.

Be brave.
Your glory
is your strength.

Isaiah 41:10; Psalm 36:7; Psalm 57:1; Malachi 4:2;
Psalm 3:3

Day 88

I hold you in the hollow of My hand.
    You can make this secret, holy place
    your home
    if you so choose.
Day and night, you may rest
    in the hollow of My hand,
    where no storm or quake can disturb.

To rest in My hand—
    this is the dream of all humankind;
    though many do not know,
    their quest for protection
    is a hunger for Me.
My hand is always open to you.
Your place with Me is safe—
    your hiding place

in My hand,
    where I want to hold you.
There is no safer place
    than this.

John 10:28; Psalm 91:9–12; 18:35; Psalm 75:8; Revelation 3:8; Isaiah 25:4

Day 89

*You will be happy and
it will be well with you.*

(Psalm 128:2b)

Come away with Me, My Beloved!
Let us laugh and be free,
   sleep and rest,
   enjoy the sounds of contentment.
What pleasure we can share!
I love not only your labor
   that you do in My name,
I love also your recreation.

Take pleasure, dearest;
   when you play as unto Me,
   play with all your heart!
Your beautiful countenance
   will be a blessing
   to all who play and rest with you.
I take joy in *all* you do,
   for when you are in need of rest,

I offer you spiritual refreshment,
physical and mental relief
in recreation.
Be light and keep your humor,
sharpen your wit,
put on your athletic prowess,
relax and enjoy.
And keep Me with you,
because I delight
in all of you—
not only in your work.

1 Timothy 6:6; Hebrews 4:3; Exodus 33:14; Matthew 11:28

Day 90

Do you not know that your body is a
temple of the Holy Spirit who is in you,
whom you have from God, and that you are
not your own?

(1 Corinthians 6:19)

Your body depends on you
    to care for its needs.
You say, "But
    'bodily exercise profiteth little.' "
You quote Me wrong.
Without exercise you cannot prosper,
    because your body will be
    neglected, lacking,
    hurting, weak—
and it is all you have
    to house your soul and spirit.

I have said you are like a tree
    planted by living waters.
Such a tree is fed,

watered, cared for.
Do not live to glorify your body,
   but live to glorify Me *in* your body.
How foolish to believe
   that exercise will harm
   the temple I have given you to use.
Find the activity which suits you.
Do all unto Me, and be glad.

Philippians 1:20; Psalm 1:3; 1 Timothy 4:7b

Day 91

*I press on toward the goal for the prize of
the upward call of God in Christ Jesus.*
(Philippians 3:14)

I have opened many doors for you to enter.
    Walk through them one by one.
Do not be discouraged
    if the blessings you hoped for
    are guarded by jealous demons
with fingers like thorns.
Do not bargain with these devils,
    or clasp their hands
in a naive effort to become friends. . . .

I will give you the grace and wisdom
    for each moment's circumstance.
Never be timid.
Never be overcome with inadequacy.
No one led by My Spirit is inadequate
    for the task I give,
Do you understand?

Learn to move, always following My direction,
    for I will never overwork you.
Open the most magnificent door of all—
    the door where I stand
    ready to embrace you.
I am accomplishing My purpose in you—
    everything you do,
    is working together for good.
We are becoming closer,
    one in our love.

Revelation 3:8; John 10:7; Psalm 1; Luke 21:15; 1 John 4:13

Day 92

Return to your rest, O my soul,
For the LORD has dealt bountifully
with you.

(Psalm 116:7)

Shall I gather all your tears
    together in one place
    and make an ocean of them?
Shall we give a name to this great,
    sad body of salty waters?
We'll call it simply *yours,*
    and it will remain as your
    ocean of tears. . . .
If you gather these tears,
    keeping them to yourself,
    they become a bitter sea.
If you give them to Me,
    I'll make them a heavenly blessing,
    asplash with lasting joy.
All earth-bound shrines
    will come to nothing,

no matter how sad.

Give your tears to Me.

Psalm 6:6; Isaiah 25:8; Psalm 116:8; 56:8

Day 93

Now therefore, O sons, listen to Me,
For blessed are they who keep My ways.
Heed instruction and be wise,
And do not neglect it.
Blessed is the man who listens to Me,
Watching daily at My gates,
Waiting at My doorposts.
For he who finds Me finds life,
And obtains favor from the LORD.
(Proverbs 8:32–35)

Divine energy is My gift to you.
This energy can be wasted
    on needless cares, unbridled temper,
    rage, and indignation.
Or, it can be multiplied
    in power and productivity.

You are master of your choices.
    You alone rule your thoughts.
If your thoughts are unbridled, unruly,

and undisciplined,
you will dissipate your energies
   on vain mind-wanderings
   and foolish emotions.
Build and multiply divine energy
   by planting good seeds of truth
   and wisdom in your mind.
That which you entertain in your secret
   thought-life will bear fruit
   either to waste or to bless.
If you choose the good seed of kindness
   you will be rewarded openly,
   and if you plant forgiveness, generosity,
   respect for all persons,
   you will reap contentment.
When you exercise your energies
   for the purposes of hope and praise,
   faith and love,
   you will always reap the rewards
of blessed spiritual satisfaction
   and inner fulfillment.

Begin to plant new seeds today.

Proverbs 10:4; 2 Timothy 1:7; 2 Corinthians 9:6–12

Day 94

*And Jesus came to them and touched them
and said, "Arise, and do not be afraid."*
(Matthew 17:7)

I have wonderful things in store for you today:
Encourage your heart.
The move of My Spirit
is as the rushing of a mighty wind.
All it touches is transformed.
You are touched and indwelt by My Spirit.
Signs and wonders are everywhere,
yet few truly believe.
Do not ever doubt My power or My love!

Many blessings, like rain falling to the earth,
are coming to you:
I hear your prayers.
I have not left you alone.
I will answer every heart-cry.
You are precious to Me,
and those you love are precious to Me.

Your loving, gracious heart has touched Mine:
    Your reasonings with Me
are proven and honorable in My sight,
    and I am telling you
I shall fulfill My Word in you.
Take heart.
Expect great things today.

Acts 2:2; Jeremiah 9:24; Revelation 8:3–4; Isaiah 1:18;
1 Kings 8:56; Psalm 62:5

Day 95

I urge you therefore, brethren, by the
mercies of God, to present your bodies a
living and holy sacrifice, acceptable to God,
which is your spiritual service of worship.
(Romans 12:1)

The discovery of joy includes
   the discovery of discipline.
Self-discipline can appear holy,
   but only to the human eye,
   not Mine.
Pause to look
   carefully into the mirror
   of the Holy Spirit:
Whose face looks back at you?
   Is it your own,
clearly painted with the colors of
   sin and ambition,
or is it the sweet reflection
   of a person at peace
with life and its circumstances?

The Holy Spirit within you
is humble, gentle—
    never full of pride or strife.

I love you,
    but My love is not indulgence.
I pamper your soul,
    but not if you oppose My will.
I answer every prayer,
    but I do not spoil you
    by catering to your old nature.
Take control of every thought;
    yield to Me.
    Discipline your mind.

Proverbs 3:11; Hebrews 9:14; Proverbs 2:11–12; Philippians 4:8; Psalm 119:24

Day 96

For to a person who is good in His sight He
has given wisdom and knowledge and joy.
(Ecclesiastes 2:26a)

Do not be hindered
    because you lack knowledge
    of My Word.
I want to speak to you of
    family, friends, children,
    and loved ones
    who are precious souls—
gifts to you from Me.

When you listen to My voice,
    you will marvel at the sweetness
    that will flood your entire being.
You will sense the presence of peace
    and confidence in the powerful touch
    of My Holy Spirit.
Though you have felt inadequate in the past,
    and though frustration has plagued you,

194

you will no longer be intimidated and overwhelmed
by your own deceptive heart.

I give you integrity:
Do not lie to protect yourself.
Do not boast to impress strangers.
You want respect, but it doesn't come cheaply.
You want love, but it isn't free of charge.
Integrity is more than vain fantasies
to be admired, adored.
Let Me live in your heart
to remove the fragments
of your crushed spirit.
I know the pain you have suffered,
and I know how you have tried
to hide from your fears—
but dear one,
you can face them.

In the humility of My love,
in the new life of My Spirit,
you have the respect you crave.

*John 17:13; Psalm 1:1–3; Proverbs 21:5–6; Proverbs 11:1;
Hebrews 13:5; 1 Thessalonians 3:12; Proverbs 16:7*

Day 97

*Beware, and be on your guard against
every form of greed; for not even when one
has an abundance does his life consist of his
possessions.*

(Luke 12:15)

The things you own
    are not as important
    as you may think.
I know what things you have need of,
    and I am concerned about
    every hair on your head.
But you are concerned
    about such things as
    what to fill your closets with.
    You lust for items in the store windows.
You burden yourself with bills
    to pay for what you have bought—
    to make yourself feel richer
    than you are.

Consider the lilies of the field, My love,
　　they neither toil nor spin,
　　and they are arrayed in beauty.
　　Even King Solomon—
the richest king in the world—
　　did not wear clothing as beautiful
　　as a single lily.

You may gather to yourself
　　real estate, investments,
　　cars, trips, jewels, gold and silver;
you may own a castle in every country;
　　you may have islands named for you.
But, oh, Beloved,
　　I am richer than these,
　　and in Me you have no lack,
　　no matter what you own.
Detach yourself from *things*
　　and see yourself as standing tall,
　　like a pillar of light and beauty,
　　rich in the glory of God's unlimited resources.
Know My mind.
　　I am greater than what you own.
　　I am more than all your wants.
There is never, nor can there ever be,
　　any exhausting of My resources.
I want you to enter the place
　　of unending riches,

where your spirit grows in honesty
    and love
and where the things you own
    do not belittle you.

Philippians 4:19; Matthew 10:30–31; Luke 12:27–28;
Proverbs 10:22; John 4:24; 6:63; Colossians 3:2

Day 98

I am with you, and will keep you wherever
you go. . . .
(Genesis 28:15a)

My hand is upon you.
    I reveal myself continually to you.
Never be discouraged.
    Never be weary of heart.
    You will reap much if you faint not.
I have many skies for you to fly,
    many valleys to ride across,
many hills to climb.
    You will love this call;
    you will love this challenge.
You will find My hand on everything you touch,
    and you will rejoice.
You will never stop being amazed
    and surprised by joy,
    never stop discovering the vastness of My heart.

I love you, dearest one.

I am your God and Lord:
    Come with Me;
bring My joy with you,
    for we are one.

Luke 18:1; Romans 12:12; Galatians 6:9; 2 Peter 1:4;
2 Corinthians 9:8; Jeremiah 31:3; 1 Peter 1:7

Day 99

*So because you are lukewarm, and neither
hot nor cold, I will spit you out of My
mouth.*

(Revelation 3:16)

There is no place in your life
   for mediocrity.
Nothing about your God is
   casual or lackluster,
   lukewarm.
If you bear the name Christian,
   you cannot walk in the world unnoticed,
   you cannot live a tepid, bland life
   without stirring My Spirit.
I am a holy God.
   I require all of you.

To know Me is to obey Me.
   In obedience to Me, you reflect
   the image of Christ.
If you do not want to live

in mediocrity,
   obey Me fully.
Open your ears,
   and let Me speak to you.
Hear how precious you are to Me.
There is no substitute
   for My love for you.
   There is no substitute
   for your love for Me.

Acts 14:3; Isaiah 30:21; Psalm 48:14

Day 100

*In everything you were enriched in Him, in
all speech and all knowledge.*

(1 Corinthians 1:5)

To whom do you look
for acceptance?
You were not put on the earth
to earn human acceptance,
but to glorify Me
in your affections and your deeds.
But you are free to choose.

If you look to people for approval,
you will compare yourself with others
and you will think in terms
of inferiority and superiority.
These do not exist in My kingdom.
Every motive in your heart and mind
must originate in Me.
Can you keep your eyes on Me?
Can you permit yourself the joy

of being fully submitted to Me?
Can you stop comparing yourself
    with others,
    and live for My glory?
Oh, the beauty and delights
    that await you!
Be My joy and enter My heart,
    and then through the discovery of joy,
go and lift and inspire others
    to the heights
you have found in Me.

Acts 10:34–35; James 2:5; 2 Corinthians 10:12; Psalm 34:3

Day 101

However, you are not in the flesh but in the Spirit, if indeed the Spirit of God dwells in you. But if anyone does not have the Spirit of Christ, he does not belong to Him.

(Romans 8:9)

There is an emotional contagion
    which takes effect
    almost unconsciously.
The spread of panic through a crowd
    is not due to independent
    frightened feelings.
Each one becomes terrified
    because another is terrified.
Fear is not the only emotion
    that is contagious.
The sight of someone in pain,
    the sound of his agony,
will produce in another
    an echo of that pain.

But, if you have a moral struggle
    and gain a moral victory—
    others will also benefit.
Victory is transmitted, too!
When you gain mastery
    over selfishness,
    or a bad habit;
when you are no longer
    spiritually sluggish,
when your captive soul is set free
    and your struggle for holiness
    is won,
    others become stronger,
    braver, better!
When you walk in the Spirit,
    when you live the life of Christ in you,
you become part of a divine "contagion"—
    It is the discovery of all joy.

Titus 2:7; Luke 22:32; Colossians 3:4; 1:27; John 6:63